But Is It Art?

Performance Art

Alix Wood

Gareth Stevens
PUBLISHING

Please visit our website, **www.garethstevens.com**. For a free color catalog of all our high-quality books, call toll free 1-800-542-2595 or fax 1-877-542-2596.

Library of Congress Cataloging-in-Publication Data

Wood, Alix.
 Performance art / Alix Wood.
   pages cm. — (But is it art?)
 ISBN 978-1-4824-2291-7 (pbk.)
 ISBN 978-1-4824-2292-4 (6 pack)
 ISBN 978-1-4824-2289-4 (library binding)
 1. Performance art—Juvenile literature. I. Title.
 NX456.5.P38W66 2015
 709.04'0755—dc23

                              2014035915

First Edition

Published in 2015 by
Gareth Stevens Publishing
111 East 14th Street, Suite 349
New York, NY 10003

© Alix Wood Books

Produced for Gareth Stevens by Alix Wood Books
Designed by Alix Wood
Editor: Eloise Macgregor

Photo credits:
Cover, 26 bottom © Bryan Derballa; 1, 5, 10, 11 bottom, 15 bottom, 21, 24, 29 © Shutterstock; 4 © celebrity wallpapers; 6 © Maljalen/Shutterstock; 7, 32 © Photobank gallery/Shutterstock; 8 Pavel L Photo and Video/Shutterstock; 9 © Alain Lauga/Shutterstock; 10 inset © Hans Namuth; 11 top © Adam Jones; 12 © Hartmut Rekort; 13 © Helga Esteb/Shutterstock; 14 © Pabkov/Shutterstock; 15 top © Frédéric; 16 © Shelby Lessig; 17 © Corbis; 18 top © Artistan/Shutterstock; 18/19 bottom © public domain; 20 © Elena Dijour/Shutterstock; 22 top © Tom Sandberg; 22 bottom © Cunningham Dance Foundation; 23 © Susanna Bolle; 25 © Alain Lauga/Shutterstock; 26 top © Everett Collection/Shutterstock; 27 © KN/Shutterstock.

Printed in the United States of America

CPSIA compliance information: Batch # CW15GS: For further information contact Gareth Stevens, New York, New York at 1-800-542-2595.

Contents

What Is Performance Art?

Performance art is a mixture of visual art and dramatic performance. Some performances are carefully thought out and follow a **script**. Others can be more **spontaneous**. The art form can happen anywhere, and be either live or performed on video. There are many different styles of performance that can all be called performance art. But can they be called art?

Performance artists want to break away from traditional art and old-fashioned ideas about what art is. They like to get their audience to think in new ways. Sometimes they achieve this by doing something very unusual, or shocking, or sometimes something simply dull, like sleeping!

Arty Fact

Performance artists involve the audience. They usually encourage audience participation or want a strong reaction from people watching.

In 1995 actress and performance artist Tilda Swinton slept for a week in a glass case outside the Serpentine Gallery, London, as a piece of performance art! The performance, entitled *The Maybe*, was repeated in 1996 in Rome and in 2013 at the Museum of Modern Art in New York.

Performance art sounds like it has to do with theater. It is usually thought of as being the direct opposite of theater, however. Performance art reacts against normal art forms.

WHAT DO YOU THINK?

It is unusual for people to be stared at while sleeping. Does doing that make us think about how **vulnerable** we are? Perhaps it helps us imagine what it is like to be a celebrity and be stared at doing everyday things? But is that art?

Performance art should include these four elements:

- time
- space
- the performer's body (or presence such as in a video)
- a relationship between the performer and the audience

In theater, a play is often set in a particular time or place. Performance art is set "now" and "here," wherever and whenever that may be.

When these boys perform these moves at different locations, each performance is unique because of the new surroundings.

Happenings

A "happening" is a term for performance art where the artists experiment with movement, sound, speech, and even smells! Happenings are difficult to describe as each one is unique. Like all performance art, an important feature is that the artist performs before a live audience.

Happenings usually encourage participation from spectators. Performers want to break down the imaginary "fourth wall" that separates the actors from their audience.

A group of performance artists in Slovenia dressed as aliens

This happening experiments with people's possible reactions to their first contact with friendly aliens.

The reaction of the audience can be a key factor in how a performance develops. This means that everyone present is a part of the event.

Flash mobs are a kind of happening. Flash mobs are usually assembled using social media. Groups of people gather, do something bizarre, and then leave again. They do it to entertain and express themselves artistically. The first successful flash mob was in Manhattan in 2003 at Macy's department store. More than 130 people went to the ninth floor rug department of the store and gathered around an expensive rug!

WHAT DO YOU THINK?

Are happenings art? Artist Allison Knowles' happening *Make a Salad* involved chopping vegetables. Set to music, the artist sliced, mixed, and tossed an enormous salad, and served it to the audience. Is that art?

Flash mobs were invented by Bill Wasik, while working at *Harper's Magazine*. He designed them as a fun social experiment to encourage people to be spontaneous.

A flash mob in Kiev, Ukraine

Arty Fact

Usually, key elements of a happening are planned, but there is plenty of room for **improvisation**. The outcome is **unpredictable**, which is part of the fun. No two performances can ever be the same!

weird and wonderful

Performance art can be strange. To make a performance memorable, artists will often do things that are out of the ordinary. Sometimes artists try to shock their audience to make an impact.

Australian performance art group Strange Fruit performs swaying on top of 14-foot (4.3 m) bendy poles combining theater, dance, and circus!

Performance artists want to leave a lasting impression on their audience. Most artists' idea of a successful performance is when it leaves the audience thinking about the performance for hours or even days afterward. The objective isn't to make the audience like the performance, but for it to be memorable.

WHAT DO YOU THINK?

Is it important for people to like art? Performance artists are happy as long as there is some relationship between them and the audience. Is it better if it is a positive relationship, or is it OK if the audience hates the performance?

This woman knitting makes you stop and wonder. She is unable to see and yet is wearing glasses. What music is she listening to on her headphones? Why is she covered in confetti? Does her performance mean anything? She is like a living piece of **surrealist** art!

Action Painting

Some artists turn the act of painting into a performance! Action painting is a style of art where paint can be smeared, splashed, or dribbled onto the paper. Artists use big movements and enjoy the physical act of applying the paint. The performance can be as important as the finished piece. Often the paper is placed on the floor so that the artist can apply paint from all sides. Artists may use unusual methods to get the paint on the paper, such as using a bottle of paint swinging from some string! Some artists use their feet, or even ride across the paper on a bicycle.

Artist Jackson Pollock dripping paint onto a canvas.

Arty Fact

Time magazine called Jackson Pollock "Jack the Dripper" because of his style of dripping paint onto his canvas! He would use sticks and syringes to apply his paint, too!

Pollock said that he had no fear of making changes or destroying any of the images in his paintings, because he believed the paintings had lives of their own. His job was to let the painting come through.

Most action paintings are **abstract** art. Abstract means that the paintings are not of recognizable objects. The paintings instead are made up using colors and shapes that aren't supposed to represent anything.

WHAT DO YOU THINK?

Do you think that abstract art is as skilled as art that represents something? It is difficult to paint a realistic image. However, now that we have cameras to record things as they are, is there any point? Is abstract art more inventive?

A piece of abstract art being designed on a wall in Brazil.

"My one-year-old could paint better than that" is what a lot of people say about action painting. What do you think? And if people like what a one-year-old creates, is that art too?

Fluxus Artists

Performance art works well when done by a group, with different people adding their own style to the work. In the 1960s there was a group of artists called Fluxus. "Fluxus" means "flow" in **Latin**. Fluxus artists blend different types of art together. Artists worked using music, the spoken word, and even architecture, or design. The Fluxus movement made people rethink what can be called art.

Fluxus performances were usually brief and simple. They often presented very ordinary events, such as brushing teeth, as art. They also presented very unusual musical performances! "Piano Activities" was a performance which ended in the complete destruction of the piano the group was playing!

WHAT DO YOU THINK?

Fluxus was against the skill, expression, and formal nature of traditional art. But can anything and everything be art? Ben Vautier, a French Fluxus artist, brushed his teeth on the street in Paris. Do you think brushing your teeth can be art?

A group of Fluxus artists performing "Piano Activities." They made music on the piano by playing it, plucking or tapping the strings, scratching, rubbing, and dropping objects on it, and even attacking it with a saw! The performance was shown on German television with the introduction "The lunatics have escaped!"

Fluxus artist George Brecht wrote "Event Scores." These were simple instructions to complete everyday tasks. They could be performed in public, private, or negatively (which meant deciding not to perform them at all!)

Performances of Brecht's "Drip Music" vary depending on the **interpretation** of the performer. One performer brought a stepladder on stage, poured water from a bucket into a watering can, climbed the stepladder, and poured the water noisily back into the bucket. He then bowed, folded up the ladder, and carried it off stage to applause!

Two examples of Brecht's Event Scores.

Drip Music (Drip Event)

For single or multiple performance.

A source of dripping water and an empty vessel are arranged so that the water falls into the vessel.

Second version: Dripping

Three Chair Events

- Sitting on a black chair. Occurrence.
- Yellow Chair. (Occurrence.)
- On (or near) a white chair. Occurrence.

The Fluxus philiosophy: Fluxus is an attitude. Fluxus creators like to see what happens when objects, sounds, images, and texts work together. Fluxus is simple and performances are brief. Fluxus is fun.

Famous Beatle John Lennon's wife Yoko Ono was a member of Fluxus. She once performed a work called "Cut Piece" in which the audience was invited to cut pieces of her clothes!

Yoko Ono

Street Performers

Many street performers could be called performance artists. Performers may dance, sing, juggle, **mime**, perform music, recite poetry, perform street theater, or even do circus acts. Do you think all of these would be classified as art, or are they simply entertainment?

Some cities encourage street performers. They are entertaining and create a happy atmosphere in a city center. Their positive influence has been known to cut crime, too!

Arty Fact

Recent studies have shown that there is less crime in areas where street musicians perform, because they make people happy. However, some criminals such as pickpockets target street performers' distracted audiences!

This newspaper-covered street artist is encouraging audience participation!

Performers often get tips of money from their audience.

Johan Lorbeer is a German street artist. He creates "still-life" performances in apparently impossible positions. In this picture he is standing in midair leaning against a wall. He will often drink from a water bottle or chat on the phone during his performance!

Lorbeer's "arm" is actually a supporting metal beam with a fake latex hand. His real arm is hidden in his sleeve. A metal bar runs down through his trousers and to platforms under his feet!

WHAT DO YOU THINK?

Are all street performers creating art? Are some of them simply entertainers? Are all the jugglers pictured below artists? Just because something is skillful doesn't make it art. Fixing a car is skillful, too, but no one thinks that's art.

Which jugglers if any do you think are creating art?

In Museums

Many artists present live performances in museums and galleries. What do you think about these two pieces? Is someone sitting silently in a chair art? What about someone painting themselves and hanging themselves in a picture frame?

The Museum of Modern Art, New York held an exhibition by Marina Abramović called "The Artist is Present." She sat completely still in a chair. In front of her was a small table and an empty chair. Spectators were invited to sit silently in the empty chair for as long as they wished and become participants in the artwork. Abramović performed every day that the museum was open between March 14 and May 31, 2010!

Arty Fact

Celebrities such as the singer Björk and actor James Franco took their turn in the empty chair during the "Artist is Present" exhibition!

A spectator takes his turn to sit opposite the artist during "The Artist is Present."

James Melloy, Stephen Taylor Woodrow, and Dale Devereux Barker hung in picture frames on a wall at a museum in New York. They wanted to explore the relationship between art and its audience. The artists shook hands with spectators and moved around!

Woodrow admitted being a painting sometimes put him in a bad mood, especially when someone offered him a snack or said something stupid!

17

On Camera

Some types of performance art are created specifically for the camera, either in the form of videos or photographs.

Filmed performance art can be viewed by many more people than would go to an art exhibition. It can also be watched many years later. The space where a work is exhibited can be important when making sense of the work, too. Some artists are happy for their work to be seen by anyone, anywhere. Some prefer to control how a work is viewed.

Not all filmed art suits being seen on a TV or computer screen. Many artists prefer to show it in a gallery space.

These photographs show a happening by performance artist Marta Minujín. Wrapped in newspaper, she read the news and then went into the river until the paper dissolved!

Performance artist Marta Minujín has said that she believes "everything is art."

Marta Minujín performing "Reading the News."

Video has been used in many creative ways. Performance artist Chantal Akerman filmed herself doing ordinary household chores around her apartment, while humming! Many artists use video within their works, even if it isn't the main medium. Minujín's "Minuphone" telephone booth allowed visitors to dial a number which triggered different events. Colors projected from glass panels, there were sounds, and the visitors' faces were displayed on a television screen in the floor!

Pipilotti Rist creates giant, room-sized video installations. They are designed to totally surround the viewer. This makes her videos only suitable to be displayed in a gallery, where they can be viewed on enormous screens.

WHAT DO YOU THINK?

Is it important for an artist to control how people view their work? If a work of art was designed to be seen on a big screen, can we judge it if we only see it on a small screen?

Create a Happening!

Performance art is fun. You could try and create your own happening. You could perform one by yourself, or get a group of friends together and create one together.

First you need to decide what kind of art you want to create. Would you rather try action painting, perform music or dance, or do something unexpected?

Decide where you want to perform your art. Where would you get the best audience? Do you need audience participation? Make sure that where you chose will be safe and that a responsible adult knows what you are planning to do.

Do you want to record your performance? Ask someone to photograph or video it, if you do.

Maybe you could stage your own pillow-fight happening? Make sure you get permission to use the pillows first!

Arty Fact

Many kids' clubs have held flash mob dance exhibitions in shopping centers and other public spaces. It can be really fun to take part. See if your local club would like to stage one.

You could try making some experimental music. Maybe get some plastic containers and some sticks, sit on the floor, and start drumming. Invite people to join you and make music. Pretty soon maybe some other people will join in and start to dance. Then you'll have a performance!

A happening can be as simple as standing in a crowded place and pointing up at the sky. Soon, other people will start to look up. If your acting skills are good enough, you may draw a crowd!

Paint yourselves into the picture! Part of the fun of action art is splashing the paint. Why not film yourselves creating your art, too?

21

Music and Silence

John Cage

John Cage was an experimental American composer. He made music using all kinds of instruments, including tape recorders, record players, and radios!

Cage thought music was not communication from the artist to the audience, but an activity where the artist lets the sounds be themselves. The sounds could open the minds of the people who made them, or who listened to them, to other possibilities they had not considered.

0' 00"

"In a situation provided with maximum amplification (no feedback), perform a disciplined action"

0' 00" was one of Cage's scores. The zeros mean unmeasured time. Cage wanted to find a way to make music not depend on time.

John Cage (on the right) performs at a festival in 1971.

4'33" is one of Cage's best known works. The piece is four minutes and 33 seconds of silence! Musicians would present the work, but do nothing apart from be present during the time period. Cage realized that there was no such thing as complete silence. The audience would be able to hear noises from their environment. The time gave the audience an opportunity to focus on the noises around them. Every performance was certainly different!

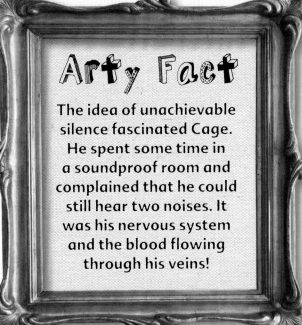

Arty Fact

The idea of unachievable silence fascinated Cage. He spent some time in a soundproof room and complained that he could still hear two noises. It was his nervous system and the blood flowing through his veins!

Cage created a "prepared piano" when the stage he had to perform a piece on had no room for any **percussion**. The only instrument available was a single grand piano. To solve the problem, he modified the piano by inserting bolts and other objects in the strings so it sounded like percussion too!

a prepared piano

WHAT DO YOU THINK?

What do you think about a piece of music that has no sound? Because an audience is expecting to hear something special, they may have a more positive point of view about the everyday noises that they do hear?

"There is no such thing as an empty space or an empty time. There is always something to see, something to hear. In fact, try as we may to make a silence, we cannot." **John Cage**

Street Theater

Street theater can take place anywhere. Actors can be either buskers performing for money, or theater groups trying out new ways of reaching people.

Performances need to be noticeable to attract a crowd in a busy street. Dance, mime, and comedy often work well. Dancing with trash cans on your head would probably draw a crowd!

WHAT DO YOU THINK?

Some theater companies like to perform street theater to reach a wider audience. Do you think seeing a street performance would encourage people to go to an actual theater?

Dancers perform at a street theater festival in France.

Street theater can be used to air political views that may not be accepted in a regular theater. Graffiti artists sometimes use their art to get political messages across to the man in the street. Street theater can be used to reach the same audience.

Mime artists mirror each others' movements during a street theater performance.

Abbie Hoffman used theatrical methods to get attention while protesting against the Vietnam war. He once wittily said "free speech is the right to shout 'theater' in a crowded fire!"

Arty Fact

Notable performers that began their careers as street theater performers include actor Robin Williams, singers David Bowie and Jewel, and actor and magician Harry Anderson.

People who might not be able to afford to go to the theater can watch a street show. The audience is made up of anyone who happens to pass by. Even if a performer is busking, the audience doesn't have to pay, it's optional. In this way art is brought to everyone. Is art that is done for free more valuable to society than traditional art? If it gets more people interested in art, and gives enjoyment, then perhaps it is?

Art or Entertainment?

Performance artist and magician David Blaine puts on incredible performances. His act is a mixture of art, magic, endurance, and entertainment. Some of his feats include being encased in a block of ice, spending days in a plastic box suspended in the air, and living in a sphere underwater!

David Blaine

David Blaine's performances are all about taking risks and going into unchartered territory. He is a showman and his stunts are always visually exciting.

David Blaine performing "Electrified." He spent 73 hours on a platform surrounded by 1 million volts of electricity! People watching could control the electricity using their computers.

David Blaine's stunts are entertainment, but are they art too? Blaine believes that to be a great magician you really need to be a good actor pretending to be a magician. The magic skills themselves are only part of the performance. He takes a lot of care organizing the presentation. For "Electrified" he drew sketches of how the set should look to give to his design team. Like many performance artists he encourages audience participation, too.

In many cities in the world street artists make themselves up to look like statues. Some, like this one on the right, are incredibly realistic. It is funny when the statue moves and takes someone by surprise! Do you think this is a mixture of art and entertainment?

WHAT DO YOU THINK?

Is all art entertainment? Is all entertainment art? Generally, entertainment makes us feel good and gives us what we want. It changes with tastes and fashions. Art is supposed to surprise us and change us. Art gives us what we didn't realize we wanted!

A living statue entertains the tourists.

Is Performance Art Art?

Have you made up your mind? Is performance art art? To help you, have a look at some of these arguments "for" and "against."

Performance Art IS Art

- Performance art is imaginative
- It can be a way for people to share their ideas
- The artists are expressing themselves
- Museums and galleries exhibit performance art
- Street performers attract tourists from around the world who like what they create
- If performance artists think what they are doing is art, then it must be

Performance Art ISN'T Art

- Some performance art is not planned but just happens. How can that be art?
- How can just sitting in a chair, for example, be art?
- Performance artists think they are anti-art, so what they produce can't be art
- Performance art is really entertainment, not art
- Silence can't be art

Performance art: Art in which the medium is the artist's own body and the artwork takes the form of actions performed by the artist.

The main purpose of performance art is almost always to challenge the conventions of traditional art such as painting and sculpture. These art forms can seem too old-fashioned, too traditional, and too distant from ordinary people. Performance artists react by using their performances to find new audiences and test new ideas.

WHAT DO YOU THINK?

Some art critics think that performance art cannot be art because it is not permanent. What do you think? Have you made up your mind? Perhaps some performance art is art, and some isn't?

Glossary

abstract
Using elements of form such as color, line, or texture with little or no attempt at creating a realistic picture.

improvisation
The act of making, inventing, or arranging on the spur of the moment or without planning.

interpretation
The act of bringing out the meaning of something by performing it in a certain way.

Latin
The language spoken in ancient Rome.

mime
The art of showing a character or telling a story by body movements.

percussion
A musical instrument such as a drum, cymbal, or maraca played by striking or shaking.

script
The written text of a stage play, screenplay, or broadcast.

spontaneous
Done, said, or produced freely and naturally without any outside cause.

surrealist
Someone who practices art that follows the surreal artistic and literary movement, dedicated to expressing the imagination as revealed in dreams, free of the conscious control of reason and convention.

unpredictable
Not able to foretell what will happen on the basis of observation, experience, or reasoning.

vulnerable
Open to attack or damage.

For More Information

Books

Bany-Winters, Lisa. *On Stage: Theater Games and Activities for Kids.* Chicago, IL: Chicago Review Press, 2012.

Oliver, Clare. *Jackson Pollock.* London, UK: Franklin Watts, 2003.

Websites

Art Smarts 4 Kids
http://artsmarts4kids.blogspot.co.uk/2007/09/jackson-pollock-and-lavender-mist.html
Information about Jackson Pollock, and some links to other great art websites.

SmART Kids
http://smartmuseum.uchicago.edu/smartkids/home.html
An interactive website that explores all kinds of art, art terms, and has a sketchbook you can write notes in!

Publisher's note to educators and parents:
Our editors have carefully reviewed these websites to ensure that they are suitable for students. Many websites change frequently, however, and we cannot guarantee that a site's future contents will continue to meet our high standards of quality and educational value. Be advised that students should be closely supervised whenever they access the Internet.

Index

discarded